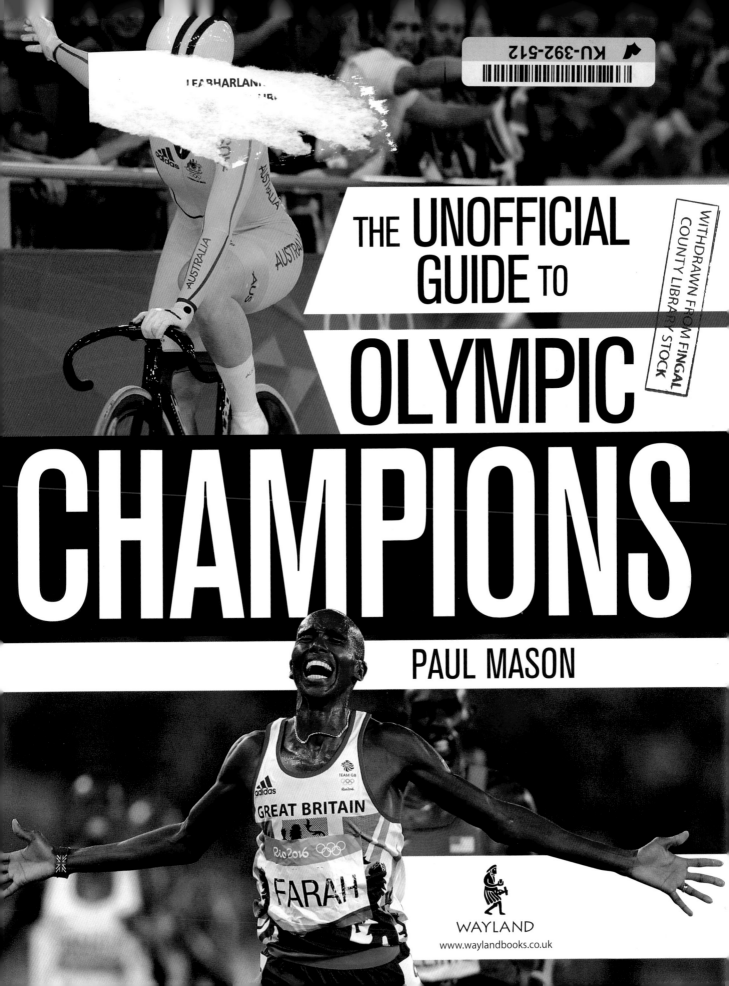

KU-392-512

WITHDRAWN FROM FINGAL
COUNTY LIBRARY STOCK

LEABHARLANN

THE UNOFFICIAL GUIDE TO OLYMPIC CHAMPIONS

PAUL MASON

GREAT BRITAIN

Rio 2016

FARAH

WAYLAND
www.waylandbooks.co.uk

First published in 2019 by Wayland
Copyright © Hodder & Stoughton, 201

Wayland
An imprint of
Hachette Children's Group
Part of Hodder and Stoughton
Carmelite House
50 Victoria Embankment
London EC4Y 0DZ

www.hachette.co.uk

Editor: Julia Bird
Design: RockJaw Creative

HB ISBN: 978 1 5263 1029 3
PB ISBN: 978 1 5263 1030 9

Printed in Dubai

FSC
www.fsc.org
MIX
Paper from
responsible sources
FSC® C104740

Please note: The statistics in this book were correct at the time of printing, but because of the nature of sport, it cannot be guaranteed that they are now accurate.

Picture credits: AFP/Getty Images: 15c. Lars Baron/Bongarts/Getty Images: 27b. Bettmann Archive/Getty Images: 29b. Clive Brunskill/Getty Images: 18bl. Gabriel Buoys/Getty Images: 8-9. Llinda Cataffo/New York Daily News/Getty Images: 9b. Robert Cianfione/FIFA via Getty Images: 14-15. Timothy Clary/Getty Images: 21t. Adrian Dennis/AFP/Getty Images: 19br. Getty Images: 4-5b. Scott Heavey/Getty Images: 10. Heinz Kluetmeier/Sports Illustrated/Getty Images: 11. Bryn Lennon/Getty Images: 23. Alex Livesey/Getty Images: 17b. Ian MacNicol/Getty Images: 13t. Buda Mendes/Getty Images: 8b. Antonov Mladen/AFP/Getty Images: 25. Olivier Morin/AFP/Getty Images: 6b. Don Morely/Getty Images: 17t. Leon Neal/AFP/Getty Images: front cover t, 1t,13b. Iuri Osadchi/Shutterstock: 24. Adam Pretty/Getty Images: 6-7, 22c. Michael Regan/Getty Images: 29t. Quinn Rooney/Getty Images: 12c. Chris Smith/Popperfoto/Getty Images: 18-19. Cameron Spencer/Getty Images: 27t. Bob Thomas Sports Photograph/Getty Images: 28b. Petr Toman/Shutterstock: 5c. Ian Walton/Getty Images: front cover b, 1b. Leonard Zhukovsky/Shutterstock: 2,16cl, 20br, 21b, 26b.

Every attempt has been made to clear copyright. Should there be any inadvertent omission please apply to the publisher for rectification.

CONTENTS

Leabharlanna Fhine Gall

'Faster, higher, stronger'

The Olympic motto is *Citius, altius, fortius* – Latin for 'Faster, higher, stronger'. This motto shows the spirit of the Olympic Games. It means that every time athletes do something, they try to do it better than ever before. Striving to be the best has led to some amazing Olympic performances.

"I didn't set out to beat the world; I just set out to do my absolute best." – Al Oerter, gold medallist in discus at the 1956, 1960, 1964 and 1968 Olympics

Four-year challenge

Even getting to the Olympics is a big achievement. You have to be one of the best athletes in your entire country. Plus, the Olympics only come round once every four years, making it even harder to qualify. Once you get to the Games, winning is even tougher. Now you are up against the best athletes in the world. Coming first is an amazing achievement and would be enough for most people. Some Olympic champions, though, have a bagful of medals.

Olympic odds

In 2016, the world's population was 7,466,964,280. At the Summer Olympics that year, 307 gold medals were awarded. This is roughly one gold for every 24.3 million people in the world! At the Winter Olympics it's even harder. There were only 103 golds at the 2018 Games, but by then the world's population had reached 7,632,819,325. That equalled one gold medal for every 74.1 million people. These challenging odds make the achievements of the sportspeople in this book even more remarkable.

Below: *A variety of starting positions for the 100 m race at the first modern Olympics held in Athens, Greece in 1896*

Below left: *The razzmatazz of the opening ceremony for the 2016 Olympics in Rio de Janeiro, Brazil*

Usain **BOLT**

Usain Bolt is probably the greatest Olympic track sprinter the world will ever see.

COUNTRY: Jamaica
BORN: 21 August 1986
EVENTS: Sprints
OLYMPIC MEDALS:
8 gold (100 m, 200 m at 2008 Olympics; 100 m, 200 m, 4 x 100 m relay at 2012 and 2016 Olympics)

The winner of the men's 100 metre sprint gets to say he is the fastest person at the Olympics. This is the Games' biggest event and Usain Bolt has won three of them in a row – an achievement that will probably never be beaten.

Late starter

Bolt was brought up in a small town in Jamaica. As a kid he played cricket and football. His cricket teacher noticed how fast Bolt was and pushed him to give athletics a try. Bolt won his first high-school championships medal (a silver) in 2001 – just seven years before his first Olympic win.

"When I was young, I didn't really think about anything other than sports." – Usain Bolt

Bolt at the Games

Bolt was the favourite in the 100 metres at the 2008 Olympics. In the final he won by 0.2 seconds – despite slowing down to celebrate and having one shoelace undone! He also won gold in the 200 metres and the 4 x 100 metres relay, making it a sprint triple.

It was an amazing achievement – but Bolt was only just getting started. In 2012, he again won all three sprint medals. Then in 2016, he did it again, becoming the only sprinter ever to win a triple triple.

In 2017, Bolt lost his amazing record. One of Jamaica's 2008 sprint relay team was found to have been using banned drugs and the team was disqualified. However, Bolt still leaves an unforgettable Olympic legacy.

Right: *Usain Bolt – so cool he can even make a dorky 'lightning bolt' pose look good.*

OLYMPIC LEGEND
Mo **FARAH**

0 **4** 0

COUNTRY: Great Britain
BORN: 23 March 1983
EVENTS: 5,000 m, 10,000 m
OLYMPIC MEDALS: 4 gold

Farah was born in Somalia, but moved to the UK when he was eight. As a boy he dreamed of playing on the wing for Arsenal Football Club, but it turned out he had different talents.

In 2012 in London, Farah won the 10,000 and 5,000 metres. It started a rush of medals for Great Britain, and Farah's 'Mobot' celebration became famous. He was doing the Mobot again four years later, after winning the 5,000 and 10,000 metres at the 2016 Games. Only one other athlete has achieved this.*

Finland's Lasse Virén, in the 1972 and 1976 Olympics.

Right: *During Mo's famous 5,000 metres win in 2012, the noise of the crowd was so great that it made the photo-finish camera shake!*

Valerie ADAMS

Dame Valerie Adams is the greatest female shot-putter in the history of the Olympics.

COUNTRY: New Zealand
BORN: 6 October 1984
EVENTS: Shot put
OLYMPIC MEDALS:
2 gold (shot-put at 2008 and 2012 Olympics), 1 silver

0 2 1

Kiwi champion

In 2008 in Beijing, Adams won New Zealand's first athletics gold at the Olympics for 22 years.* She lost her crown four years afterwards – but was later awarded the gold. At the 2016 Olympics, Adams had a chance to make history.

Rotorua childhood

Adams was born in the town of Rotorua, New Zealand. As a youngster she was teased for her size, but Adams outgrew the bullying. She started shot-put when she was only ten, smashing a 20-year-old school record. By the time of her first Olympics Adams had won world titles at youth, junior and senior levels.

Above: *Valerie Adams celebrates her silver medal in the 2016 Olympics.*

Olympic glory

In 2008, Adams was up against two athletes from Belarus: Nadzeya Ostapchuk and Natalya Mikhnevich.** She out-threw both of them to win. At the next Games, in 2012, Ostapchuk threw 36 cm further than Adams. Then it was announced the Belarusian had been caught doping. The gold medal belonged to Adams!

2016: the final test

At the 2016 Olympics, Adams was on the brink of history. Only one other shot-putter had ever won two golds: Tamara Press of the USSR, in 1960 and 1964. No one had ever won three. Adams was leading before the last round of throws. Then, Michelle Carter of the USA threw 21 cm further. Adams finished with silver, but still became the most successful female shot-putter ever.

*The last had been John Walker in the 1,500 m at the 1976 Olympics.
**Both later disqualified for doping.

OLYMPIC LEGEND
Carl **LEWIS**

0 9 1

COUNTRY: USA
BORN: 1 July 1961
EVENTS: Sprints, long jump
OLYMPIC MEDALS: 9 gold, 1 silver

Carl Lewis was the athlete to beat during the 1980s and early 1990s – and not many people could beat him. Between 1984 and 1992 he sprinted to five Olympic golds. He set several world records, and in the 4 x 100 m relay in 1992 he ran 8.85 seconds – the fastest anchor leg ever recorded.

The thing is, sprinting wasn't even Lewis' best event …

In 1984, 1988, 1992 and 1996, Lewis won Olympic gold at the long jump. He was 23 years old when he won the first medal, and 35 when he won the last.

Above: *Carl Lewis leaps into the lead at the 1996 Olympics.*

Nicola ADAMS

Nicola Adams holds one Olympic record that will definitely NEVER be beaten. In 2012 she became history's first female Olympic boxing champion.

COUNTRY: Great Britain
BORN: 26 October 1982
EVENTS: Flyweight boxing
OLYMPIC MEDALS:
2 gold (flyweight 2012 and 2016)

0 2 0

Finding a way

Adams started boxing when she was 12 years old. At the time, women's boxing was officially banned in the UK and many other places.

At 13 Adams won her first fight, but it took four years for her to find another opponent. She won that next fight too, and kept winning. In 2009 women's boxing became an Olympic sport. Adams set her sights on striking gold at the 2012 Olympics.

2012: Adams v. Ren

After winning in the quarter- and semi-finals, Adams met the Chinese boxer Ren Cancan in the Olympic final. Ren was a three-time world champion, current world number one and had beaten Adams in the last two world championships. Even so, Adams dominated. She won the first round 4–2, knocked Ren down in round 2, and ended the fight 16–7 ahead. Gold!

2016: aiming for the double

At the 2016 Olympics in Brazil, Adams was the favourite to win. She had just won a world championship and was boxing better than ever. After beating her old rival Ren in the semi-final, Adams was up against France's Sarah Ourahmoune in the final. She was rarely threatened and won by a long way. Gold again!

"I loved it when people said I boxed like a boy. It gave me a lot of confidence and street cred."
– Nicola Adams

Right: Nicola Adams wheels away in triumph after winning the first women's boxing Olympic gold medal.

Teófilo **STEVENSON**

Only one Olympic boxer ever managed to finish a fight against Teófilo Stevenson.

COUNTRY: Cuba
BORN: 29 March 1952
EVENTS: Heavyweight boxing
OLYMPIC MEDALS:
3 gold (heavyweight 1972, 1976, 1980)

0 3 0

Below: Teófilo Stevenson (right) spars his way to victory in the 1980 Olympics.

Dad's the word

The story goes that when Stevenson's mum found out her nine-year-old son had been training at the boxing gym, she was furious. She did eventually say he could go, as long as his dad took him. Fortunately, it was his dad who had secretly been taking him all along.

Triple gold

Stevenson won gold at three Olympics*, starting in 1972. In 1976 he won his first three fights so quickly that each opponent lasted an average of just 2 minutes and 27 seconds. Having fought for less than seven-and-a-half minutes, Stevenson was fresh for his last fight, the final. In the circumstances Mircea Şimion of Romania did well to make it to round three before his corner decided to throw in the towel.

*Only one other boxer has done this, László Papp of Hungary in 1948, 1952 and 1956.

Champion again

In 1980 someone finally lasted until the end of an Olympic fight with Stevenson. István Lévai of Hungary spent the whole of the semi-final running away. He still lost. Stevenson went on to beat Pyotr Zayev in the final to become Olympic champion for a third time.

In 1984 Cuba boycotted the Olympics and Stevenson did not fight. He had beaten the new Olympic champion, Tyrell Biggs, just months before. If he had been at the Games, Stevenson might well have won a fourth gold.

"I have never been hit so hard in all my 212 bouts. You don't see his right hand. All of a sudden it is there – on your chin."
– Peter Hussing of Germany, knocked out in the second round by Teófilo Stevenson at the 1972 Olympics

Jason KENNY

Jason Kenny is Britain's [joint] most successful Olympic cyclist, with six gold medals.

COUNTRY: Great Britain
BORN: 23 March 1988
EVENTS: Team sprint, individual sprint, keirin
OLYMPIC MEDALS:
6 gold (team sprint 2008, 2012, 2016; individual sprint 2012, 2016; keirin 2016), 1 silver

0   6   1

Cycling champions

Picking Britain's most successful Olympic cyclist is not easy. Kenny is actually tied with Chris Hoy on six golds. Bradley Wiggins has won more medals with five gold, one silver and two bronze. And Laura Kenny, Jason's wife, has won four golds. If Kenny races at the 2020 Olympics in Japan, though, he has the chance to break all the records.

Fast learner

Kenny only started racing a bike on the track when he was 15 years old. Within three years he was the European and world champion. Two years later Kenny was chosen to go to the 2008 Olympics.

2008: team-sprint glory

Medal one came in the team sprint, where three cyclists ride three laps as fast as possible. Each rider does one lap in the lead, then drops away. The last lap is done by one rider alone. Kenny, Jamie Staff and Chris Hoy won gold, breaking the world record in the process. Two days later, Kenny won silver behind Hoy in the individual sprint race.

2012: battle with Baugé

Between 2008 and the 2012 Games, Kenny lost almost every race he had with the great French rider Grégory Baugé. When the two lined up in the final of the individual sprint, many expected Baugé to win again.

The individual sprint is a best-of-three contest. In the first race Kenny started on the outside, giving him an advantage: he was able to sprint past Baugé on the finishing straight. In race two, Kenny was on the inside. With a lap to go, he began to hit top speed. Baugé came flying up behind on the last bend and seemed sure to get

Opposite: Jason Kenny sprints to victory in the keirin at the 2016 Olympics.

Left: British cycling greats Jason Kenny (right) and Chris Hoy at the Beijing Olympics in 2008

past – but Kenny accelerated and just managed to win. At the same Games he also won gold in the team sprint.

2016: keirin racer

At the 2016 Olympics, Kenny tackled the keirin. In this strange race, riders do 5.5 laps behind a moped called a derny. No one is allowed to overtake the derny. Its speed increases until it pulls in and the riders race the last 2.5 laps at their own speed.

The 2016 final had to be restarted twice, after riders overtook the derny. As they hurtled towards the finish, five riders were packed tightly together. At the front was Kenny. He added gold to the individual and team sprints he had already won, making six Olympic golds in total.

OLYMPIC LEGEND
Anna **MEARES**

3 2 1

COUNTRY: Australia
BORN: 21 September 1983
EVENTS: 500 m time trial, individual sprint,
team sprint, keirin
OLYMPIC MEDALS: 2 gold, 1 silver, 3 bronze

Meares is a legendary Australian bike racer. She took up track cycling aged 11, even though the local club was 300 km away.

At her first Olympics, in 2004, Meares won gold in the 500 metre time trial and bronze in the sprint. Months before the 2008 Olympics Meares had a terrible accident, breaking her neck. Amazingly she made it to the Games and raced to silver behind Victoria Pendleton in the sprint final.

In 2012 Meares battled with Pendleton again in the sprint, this time taking gold, and won bronze in the team sprint. She followed this with a keirin bronze at the 2016 Games. She became the only Australian ever to win individual medals at four Olympics in a row.

Above: *Anna Meares celebrates after winning gold in the 2012 Olympic women's sprint.*

USA

No other team comes close to the USA's women's football team's record at the Olympics.

COUNTRY: USA
FIRST OLYMPICS: 1996
OLYMPIC MEDALS:
4 gold (1996, 2004, 2008, 2012), 1 silver

0 4 1

Winning formula

Women's football first became part of the Olympics in 1996. Between then and 2016, there were six Olympic football competitions. The USA won four of them and came second in one of the others. Along the way the team set all kinds of records that may never be beaten.

1996: women's football takes off

The 1996 Olympics were held in Atlanta, USA. The USA came second in their group behind China. They played Norway in the semi-final. After 90 minutes the score was 1–1, so the teams played extra time. The first team to score would win, a rule called the 'golden goal'. In the 100th minute, the midfielder Shannon MacMillan smashed home a goal. The USA was through to the final – against China.

In the final, MacMillan scored again after 19 minutes, then China got a goal back. As the crowd roared them on, the USA attacked and their forward Tiffeny Milbrett scored. China could not get another goal and so the USA team became the first ever female Olympic football champions.

2004–2012: winning run

At the 2000 Olympics, USA made it to the final. They faced Norway, who got revenge for 1996 by beating them 3–2. In 2004, though, the USA kicked off an amazing run of Olympic victories:

- **2004: USA 2–1 Brazil** The match finished in extra time, when Abby Wambach scored the winner after 112 minutes of play.
- **2008: Brazil 0–1 USA** Again the teams played extra time, with Carli Lloyd scoring the only goal after 96 minutes.
- **2012: USA 2–1 Japan** This match did finish on time, though Japan were very unlucky not to win a penalty – which could have made the score 2–2 – after a handball by the USA's Tobin Heath.

Right: USA striker Carli Lloyd, who scored in both 2008 and 2012 Olympic gold-medal matches.

OLYMPIC LEGEND
HUNGARY

0 3 0

COUNTRY: Hungary
FIRST OLYMPICS: 1912
OLYMPIC MEDALS: 3 gold

During the 1950s the Hungary team created a revolution in world football. They played in an exciting new way, with players swapping positions. At the heart of the team was the striker Ferenc Puskás. At the 1952 Olympics Puskás scored four goals – including one in the final against Yugoslavia.

Above: Hungary and Real Madrid star player Ferenc Puskás.

In the 1964 Olympics Hungary scored goal after goal. Their results on the way to the final included wins of 6–0, 6–5, 2–0 and 6–0. In the gold-medal match they beat Czechoslovakia 2–1 and became Olympic champions again.

Hungary also won the 1968 Olympic football contest. They had one tricky match on the way to the final, a 1–0 victory over Guatemala. In the final against Bulgaria they won easily, 4–1.

Simone **BILES**

The USA's top gymnast, Simone Biles, is a hero to young people all around the world.

COUNTRY: USA
BORN: 14 March 1997
KEY EVENTS: Floor, vault
OLYMPIC MEDALS: 4 gold (floor, vault, all-around, team 2016), 1 bronze

Opposite: Simone Biles in complete control on the balance beam.

A tough start

Biles had a tough start in life. Her mother and father were both addicted to drugs and alcohol and could not care for their four children. When she was three, Biles moved to live with her grandfather. He and his wife later adopted her and her younger sister, Adria.

Dedication and training

Simone first tried gymnastics when she was six and at eight began to train with the famous coach Aimee Boorman. In 2012 Biles decided to become home-schooled, which meant she could increase her gymnastics training from 20 to 32 hours a week. By 2013 her work was being rewarded and she won her first world championship golds. She won four golds at each of the next two world championships, in 2014 and 2015. The stage was set for the 2016 Olympics in Brazil.

The 2016 Olympics

As current world champion at three individual events, Biles was the hot favourite to win gold at the 2016 Games. Qualification for the finals went well, and she was top scorer in the all-around, vault, floor and balance beam. She had a busy few days ahead:

Above: Simone Biles proudly shows off her gold medal after winning the women's all-around competition in Rio.

"I'm not the next Usain Bolt or Michael Phelps: I'm the first Simone Biles." – Simone Biles after winning four golds at the 2016 Olympics

9 AUGUST:
Team final
Biles is the only US gymnast to take part in all four events (vault, bars, beam and floor).
Result: gold number 1

11 AUGUST:
All-around final
Undefeated in all-around competition since 2013, Biles never looks like losing and wins by 2.1 points, a huge margin.
Result: gold number 2.

14 AUGUST:
Vault final
Coming into the last vaults of the competition, Biles needed a big score. She got it: 15.966 points.
Result: gold number 3.

15 AUGUST:
Balance beam final
The only wobble of Biles' Olympics, as she slips on the beam and loses a big part of her score.
Result: bronze

16 AUGUST:
Floor final
A great performance of her samba floor routine sends the (mainly Brazilian) crowd wild. Some of her tumbles are electric.
Result: gold number 4.

OLYMPIC LEGEND
Nadia **COMANECI**

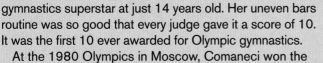

COUNTRY: Romania
BORN: 12 November 1961
KEY EVENTS: All-around, balance beam
OLYMPIC MEDALS: 5 gold

At the 1976 Olympics, Nadia Comaneci became the first gymnastics superstar at just 14 years old. Her uneven bars routine was so good that every judge gave it a score of 10. It was the first 10 ever awarded for Olympic gymnastics.

At the 1980 Olympics in Moscow, Comaneci won the balance beam and floor golds. On the floor, she drew with the Russian gymnast Nellie Kim. Comaneci's coach felt she had been marked harshly and protested, but the result stood.

Above: Comaneci's score was so unexpected that the scoreboard wasn't even able to show it properly!

Steve **REDGRAVE**

Redgrave is a legendary champion for winning gold medals at five Olympics in a row.

COUNTRY: Great Britain
BORN: 23 March 1962
EVENTS: Coxed four, coxless pair, coxless four
OLYMPIC MEDALS: 5 gold (coxed four 1984; coxless pair 1988, 1992, 1996; coxless four 2000), 1 bronze

1   5   0

River childhood

Redgrave was born near Marlow, a small town beside the River Thames. Rowing is a popular sport in the area. But as a child, Redgrave says that he dreamed of playing in the FA Cup final, not rowing at the Olympics!

To cox or not to cox?

In rowing, races are either 'coxed' or 'coxless'. (The cox is a non-rower who guides the crew.) Redgrave's first Olympic gold was in 1984 in the coxed four.

For the 1988 Games, Redgrave specialised in the coxless pair. He and Andy Holmes won gold. It was the start of an amazing run of gold medals in this event. In 1992 Redgrave won again, this time with Matthew Pinsent. He and Pinsent won the next three world championships, then won Olympic gold again in 1996.

Coxless four

After 1996, Redgrave gave up rowing and announced: 'Anybody who sees me in a boat has my permission to shoot me.' He soon changed his mind, though, and started training for the next Olympics. At the 2000 Games he raced in the coxless four alongside Pinsent, Tim Foster and James Cracknell. As the boats neared the finish Great Britain was in first place, being chased down by Italy, Australia and Slovenia. With 100 metres to go Italy made a last push for the win – but Britain held them off by 0.38 seconds. Redgrave had won gold number five.

Left: Redgrave, Foster, Cracknell and Pinsent celebrate their 2000 Olympics win.

Right: Redgrave and Andy Holmes compete at the 1988 Olympics.

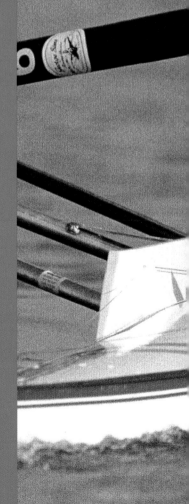

OLYMPIC LEGEND
Michal **MARTIKÁN**

1 **2** **2**

COUNTRY: Slovakia
BORN: 18 May 1979
EVENTS: Canoe slalom
OLYMPIC MEDALS: 2 gold,
2 silver, 1 bronze

Michal Martikán was the first person from Slovakia ever to win an Olympic gold medal, at the 1996 Olympics. But Martikán is legendary for another reason: his determination to win another gold.

At the 2000 and 2004 Games, the best Martikán could manage was second place. In 2008, twelve years after his first gold, he was determined to succeed. Martikán was fastest in heats, semi-final and final – and finally won a second gold.

Right: *Martikán paddles his way to a second gold medal at the 2008 Olympics in Beijing.*

Michael **PHELPS**

Swimmer Michael Phelps is the most successful Olympic champion ever with 23 Olympic golds.

COUNTRY: USA
BORN: 30 June 1985
KEY EVENTS: multiple
OLYMPIC MEDALS:
23 gold, 3 silver, 2 bronze

Dipping in

Phelps was born in Baltimore, Maryland, USA and started swimming when he was seven. One story says that he was scared to put his face in the water, so learned backstroke first. It wasn't long before he was swimming the other strokes too.

First Olympics

In 2000, when he was only 15 years old, Phelps was selected for the US Olympic swim team. At the Games he came fifth in the 200 metres butterfly, which most 15-year-old swimmers would be very pleased with. Phelps, though, wasn't 100 per cent happy: 'It was great, I was fifth, that's a pretty big accomplishment. But … I was within half a second of [a medal]'. At the next Games, fifth would not be good enough.

History maker

Phelps went on to win six gold medals at the 2004 Olympics – but he was only just warming up. At the 2008 Games he was in the best form of his life:

Right: Phelps celebrates one of his final golds, from the 4 x 100 metre medley relay in 2016.

- he qualified for eight events and won eight gold medals
- in seven events he set new world record times
- in the one non-world-record swim, the 100 metres butterfly, Phelps broke the Olympic record.

Phelps had now won 14 gold medals, more than any other Olympic athlete.

London 2012 and Rio 2016

At the 2012 Olympics Phelps won the 100 metres butterfly and 200 metres medley at the third Olympics in a row. No one had ever done this before. With two relay golds as well, he now had 18 in total. Phelps announced that he was giving up swimming – but changed his mind and decided to go for one more Olympics. At Rio, Phelps added five more gold medals, setting a record of 23 in total that will probably never be beaten.

Opposite: Michael Phelps powers through the water in the 200 m butterfly final at the 2016 Olympics in Rio de Janeiro.

OLYMPIC LEGEND
Rebecca **ADLINGTON**

COUNTRY: Great Britain
BORN: 7 Feb 1989
KEY EVENTS: 400 m and 800 m freestyle
OLYMPIC MEDALS: 2 gold, 2 bronze

Adlington learnt to swim when she was three and started racing when she was nine. In her teens she trained in the pool for 20 hours a week, swimming about 10 km a day.

At the start of 2008, few people had heard of Adlington, but all that would change at the Olympic Games. In the 800 metres she broke the oldest record in swimming, set by Janet Evans of the USA in 1989 – the year Adlington was born. She won gold by six seconds, and collected a second gold in the 400 metres.

Four years later at the London Olympics, Adlington won bronze medals in the same events. The winner of both was an Olympic legend of the future: Katie Ledecky.

"That's truly what I always dreamed of as a kid … doing something that no one had ever done before."
– Michael Phelps

Alistair **BROWNLEE**

Alistair Brownlee is the most successful Olympic champion in one of the Games' toughest events.

COUNTRY: Great Britain
BORN: 23 April 1988
EVENTS: Triathlon
OLYMPIC MEDALS: 2 gold (2012, 2016)

0 2 0

Early success

Alistair's dad was a runner and his mum was a swimmer. When he was a boy Brownlee was a good cross-country and fell runner. Then his uncle introduced him to triathlon. Brownlee was a natural and in 2006, at 18 years old, he won the world junior championship. It convinced him to give up his studies to focus on sport. Two years later he came 12th at the 2008 Olympics.

2012: home Games

The 2012 Olympics were held in London and Brownlee was desperate to win. But a few months before, he injured his Achilles tendon. He was only able to get back into full training six weeks before the Games.

After the swim section of the race he was in the leading group. He and his brother Jonny, also a top triathlete, stayed near the front during the bike ride. The winner would be decided on the run. Alistair, Jonny and Spain's Javier Gomez were soon at the front, battling for the medals. Roared on by the crowd, Alistair pulled clear, winning by 11 seconds. Gomez was second, Jonny third.

2016: the double

At the 2016 Olympics, the Brownlee brothers dreamed of doing even better than in 2012. In the swim, Alistair finished fourth. After the bike ride he was second. Jonny was close behind him all the way. The two headed off on the run, where they slowly built a lead. On the final lap, Jonny fell slowly behind. Alistair crossed the line six seconds ahead to win.

OLYMPIC LEGEND
Simon **WHITFIELD**

1 1 0

COUNTRY: Canada
BORN: 16 May 1975
EVENTS: Triathlon
OLYMPIC MEDALS: 1 gold (2000), 1 silver

Simon Whitfield was not one of the favourites in the first ever Olympic triathlon in 2000. But, after being delayed by a bike crash and starting the run in 24th place, he worked his way back towards the front. With 1 km to run, only Germany's Stephan Vuckovic was ahead. With 450 m to go, Whitfield started to sprint. He passed Vuckovic 200 m from the finish and won.

In 2008 Whitfield almost did it again, coming from fourth to first with 200 m to go. But he was then overtaken himself by the German athlete Jan Frodeno and won silver.

Right: Simon Whitfield crosses the line to become the first Olympic triathlon champion.

Right: Alistair and Jonny Brownlee fight their way uphill during the 2016 Olympics.

"When Jonny crossed the line, I said to him, 'We've done it' … To see your little brother come over the line a few seconds after you is phenomenal." – Alistair Brownlee after winning his second Olympic triathlon title

Ireen WÜST

Ireen Wüst has competed in four Winter Olympics and won gold medals at all of them. No one else has done this.

COUNTRY: the Netherlands
BORN: 1 April 1986
EVENTS: Speed skating
OLYMPIC MEDALS: 5 gold, 5 silver, 1 bronze

Ice queen

Although she only started skating when she was 11, Wüst was racing at international level by the time she was 17. Two years later, she was racing at the 2006 Winter Olympics. She won gold at the leg-burning 3,000 metres event, then bronze in the 1,500 metres. She was named 2006's Dutch Sportswoman of the Year.

More medals

At the 2010 Olympics, Wüst won the 1,500 metres. Then in 2014 she won more medals than any other athlete at the Winter Olympics, in any sport. She won gold in the 3,000 metres and team pursuit, and silver in the 1,000, 1,500 and 5,000 metres.

Four years later, Wüst said the 2018 Olympics would be her last. In the 3,000 metres and team pursuit she could only manage silver. In the 1,500 metres Wüst was one of the first to go and had to watch as everyone tried to beat her time. In the last race was Japan's Miho Takagi, unbeaten all year. Takagi set fast times on each lap, but slowed down slightly at the end. Wüst had won – by 0.2 seconds.

"Even when I watch the race today, I still can't believe that I did it. It was an amazing feeling."
– Ireen Wüst speaking about the 2006 Olympics

Above: *Irene Wüst races in the 5,000 metres during the 2014 Winter Olympics.*

Yuzuru **HANYU**

Yuzuru Hanyu is one of the greatest figure skaters of all time. He has been given world record scores 12 times.

COUNTRY: Japan
BORN: 7 December 1994
EVENTS: Figure skating
OLYMPIC MEDALS: 2 gold
(2014, 2018)

0 2 0

Young talent

Hanyu started ice skating when he was just four. When he was ten he entered Japan's novice championship and won. His local ice rink then closed, making it hard to train. It reopened three years later. Soon after, Hanyu won Japan's junior national championship at 13 years old – the youngest ever winner.

Record-breaker

By 2014 Hanyu was the world's best male figure skater. He was the first to score more than 100 points in the short programme, which is half of a figure skating contest. At the 2014 Winter Olympics he scored a world record 101.45 points. He added 178.64 points in the free skating, which was enough for gold.

Before the 2018 Olympics in Pyeongchang, South Korea, Hanyu was injured. He had only been in three contests by the time the Games began. It did not show. In his short programme he scored 111.68 points. In the free skating he scored 206.17. His routine included four quadruple jumps, in which he span around in the air four times. Hanyu had won gold again.

Right: Yuzuru Hanyu performs what looks like an impossible turn at the 2018 Winter Olympics.

Shaun WHITE

Shaun White became a legend at the 2018 Winter Olympics.

COUNTRY: USA
BORN: 3 September 1986
KEY EVENTS: Snowboard halfpipe
OLYMPIC MEDALS: 3 gold (snowboard halfpipe, 2006, 2010, 2018)

0   3   0

Skater boy
White comes from the beach city of San Diego in California, USA. Like many great snowboarders, he's also a top-level skateboarder. White started snowboarding when he was just six. By the age of seven he was entering snowboarding contests.

First Olympics
White was one of the world's best snowboarders when he went to the 2006 Winter Olympics in Turin, Italy. Qualifying for the final is decided after two runs. White's first was a disaster: he fell and scored 37.7. In his second run he managed 45.3 – enough to get through. In the final White's score of 46.8 won him gold.

The Tomahawk
At the next Olympics, White put on an amazing display. In his final run he did a trick only he could do, named the Tomahawk. It is a double McTwist 1260: a spin three-and-a-half-times around, while going upside-down backwards. The result: gold medal number two.

2014 disaster
The 2014 Winter Olympics were a disaster for White. He had the highest score in qualifying, but took risks and fell – twice – in his first run in the finals. He rode more safely in the second run and finished fourth.

Right: Shaun White celebrates his final Olympic gold, at the 2018 Games.

2018 test
In 2018 White was back at the Games. Months before, he had had a terrible crash in training. He landed on his face and needed 62 stitches.

Before the last run, White was in second place, behind Ayumu Hirano of Japan. This time he took big risks, twice spinning around in the air four times. It was enough. He edged ahead of Hirano and won a third gold.

Opposite: *Marit Bjørgen has won so many Winter Olympic medals that she is joint 28th on the list of most successful countries at the Games.*

Right: Shaun White's final run at the 2010 Games scored 48.4, the highest ever in Olympic halfpipe.

OLYMPIC LEGEND
MARIT **BJØRGEN**

3 **8** **4**

COUNTRY: Norway
BORN: 21 March 1980
EVENTS: Cross-country skiing
OLYMPIC MEDALS: 8 gold, 4 silver, 3 bronze

Many people say you have to be fitter for cross-country skiing than any other Olympic event. If this is true, Marit Bjørgen must be the fittest Olympic athlete ever. She has won more Winter Olympics gold medals than any other athlete, at any sport.

Bjørgen won her first medal, a silver, at the 2002 Olympics when she was 21 years old. Her first golds were in 2010, when she won three. In 2014 she again won three golds. And in 2018, at the age of 37, she won two more. In total Bjørgen has won an amazing 15 Winter Olympics medals.

Olympic not-so-champions

Unfortunately, in any competition there is often someone who cheats. These are a few of the worst Olympic cheats ever.

East German lugers

At the 1968 Winter Olympics, East Germany's female luge racers were almost unbeatable. They came first, second and fourth in different events.

Then it was discovered that they had been applying chemicals to the runners of their luges to heat them up. The heated runners melted the ice more than normal, resulting in faster times. The whole team was disqualified.

Fred Lorz

The crowd went wild when the marathon runner Fred Lorz came into the stadium first at the 1904 Olympics. Lorz was American, and an American winner was just what they wanted.

Unfortunately it emerged that Lorz had only actually run nine miles (15 km). His trainer had driven him another 11. When their car broke down, Lorz walked the rest of the way to the stadium.

Below left: *Johnson crosses the line ahead of Carl Lewis (in red) and Britain's Linford Christie.*

Below right: *Cheating Russian fencer Boris Onischenko contemplates how much trouble he's going to be in when he gets home.*

Ben Johnson

Johnson stunned the world when he smashed Carl Lewis (see page 9) in the 100 metres at the 1988 Olympics. His time of 9.79 seconds was a new world record.

Three days later it was announced that Johnson had tested positive for performance-enhancing drugs. He was disqualified and Lewis was promoted to gold medal position.

To prove that he was a really determined cheater, Johnson was caught using drugs AGAIN in 1993 and banned from athletics for life.

Below: *China's Yu Yang (left) and Xiaoli Wang (right) play in the women's doubles at the 2012 Olympics.*

Various badminton teams

Eight players from China, Indonesia and South Korea were banned for cheating at the 2012 Olympics.

China planned to lose some of their matches so that they would face easier opponents in later ones. The Indonesian and South Koreans realised what was happening and started losing some of THEIR matches on purpose too, as a way of blocking the Chinese plan.

In the end, none of them won.

Boris Onischenko

Onischenko (left) was a Russian pentathlete who had an amazing ability at fencing. He seemed able to score a point so quickly it could not be seen with the naked eye.

Then it was discovered that Onischenko's ability wasn't that amazing after all. He had rigged up a switch to press and score a point without actually hitting his opponent. Boris was sent home from the 1976 Olympics to have a hard think about what he'd done.

Tunisian pentathletes

Tunisia's pentathlon team got off to a bad start at the 1960 Olympics, when they all fell off their horses in the equestrian competition. Then one nearly drowned in the swimming. In the shooting contest a team member was disqualified after nearly shooting a judge (by accident). At this point they hadn't cheated, they'd just been rubbish at pentathlon.

In the fencing, though, the Tunisians only had one person who could fence. They just sent him out every time, with his mask already on, and hoped no one would notice. Someone did, though, and they were disqualified.

Olympic words

adopt become the parent of someone who is not your birth child

anchor leg last part of a relay race; the person who runs the anchor leg is the one who crosses the finish line

banned not allowed

boycott refuse to go to an event or place as a protest. In 1980 the USA and some of its allies boycotted the Olympic Games in Moscow. In 1984 the USSR and allies boycotted the Los Angeles Olympics

cox non-rower who sits at the back of the boat and guides the crew, giving them instructions on speed and steering

Czechoslovakia country that separated into two countries in 1993, the Czech Republic and Slovak Republic

disqualified removed from the results because of having broken the rules

doping taking drugs that are not allowed, as a way of getting an unfair advantage over your competitors

equestrian to do with horses

extra time extra bit of play added to a match with no winner, giving the sides a bit more time to win

favourite person considered most likely to win a competition that is about to happen

fell runner person who runs off-road in hilly countryside

finishing straight final, straight bit of athletics track leading to the finish line

form how well an athlete is doing at a particular time. Winning every race in the best time you have ever done shows you are in good form

group in knockout competitions, teams/players are usually separated into groups (often, groups of four). Everyone in the group plays everyone else, and the best two advance to the next stage

heat first round of a competition, to decide who gets into the semi-finals or final

high bar piece of gymnastic equipment (or 'apparatus'), a thin bar high above the ground, which the gymnast swings around

host city a city chosen as the venue for an Olympic Games

home games Olympic Games held in the country an athlete comes from

meet competition

novice person doing something for the first time

performance-enhancing drugs drugs that help an athlete become fitter, stronger, faster or better in some other way. Most performance-enhancing drugs are banned

podium platform on which the top three finishers stand to be given their medals

qualify be allowed to take part

regatta competition for boats, particularly sailing or rowing boats

run in halfpipe snowboarding, competitors go twice. Each go is called a 'run'

runners on a luge, sled or toboggan, the runners are the part that actually slides along the ice or snow

throw in the towel give up. In boxing, a fighter's trainer signals that the fight should be stopped by literally throwing a towel into the ring

triple collection of three wins at similar events. For example, winning the 100 metres, 200 metres and 4 x 100 metre relay is a sprinting triple

USSR Union of Soviet Socialist Republics, a country with Russia at its heart, which split up in 1991

Yugoslavia country that in 1991–92 split into several smaller ones, including Bosnia and Herzegovina, Croatia and Serbia

Olympic host cities

SUMMER OLYMPICS

1896 Athens

1900 Paris

1904 St Louis

1908 London

1912 Stockholm

1920 Antwerp

1924 Paris

1928 Amsterdam

1932 Los Angeles

1936 Berlin

1948 London

1952 Helsinki

1956 Melbourne

1960 Rome

1964 Tokyo

1968 Mexico City

1972 Munich

1976 Montreal

1980 Moscow

1984 Los Angeles

1988 Seoul

1992 Barcelona

1996 Atlanta

2000 Sydney

2004 Athens

2008 Beijing

2012 London

2016 Rio de Janeiro

2020 Tokyo

WINTER OLYMPICS

1924 Chamonix

1928 St. Moritz

1932 Lake Placid

1936 Garmisch Partenkirchen

1948 St Moritz

1952 Oslo

1956 Cortina d'Ampezzo

1960 Squaw Valley

1964 Innsbruck

1968 Grenoble

1972 Sapporo

1976 Innsbruck

1980 Lake Placid

1984 Sarajevo

1988 Calgary

1992 Albertville

1994 Lillehammer

1998 Nagano

2002 Salt Lake City

2006 Turin

2010 Vancouver

2014 Sochi

2018 Pyeongchang

Leabharlanna Fhine Gall

Index

Further information

Books

The Olympics Ancient to Modern: A Guide to the History of the Games Joe Fullman (Wayland, 2016) and *The Olympics: Going for Gold: A Guide to the Summer Games* Joe Fullman (Wayland, 2015)
These books give you the low-down on Olympic history and sports, including the new sports that will be part of the Games for the first time in 2020.

Dream to Win: Usain Bolt Roy Apps (Franklin Watts, 2016)
The story of how young Usain Bolt became a multiple Olympic champion.

Olympic Expert Paul Mason (Franklin Watts, 2016)
A guide to the different events at the Olympics, peppered with fun facts about subjects like the Olympic tug-of-war, the biggest sulk in Olympic history and much more.

Websites

The International Olympic Committee site has background information and photos of many top Olympic athletes – check it out here: *www.olympic.org/athletes*

The US broadcaster NBC has compiled a list ranking the top 100 Olympic athletes of all time – see whether you agree! *sportsworld.nbcsports.com/the-top-100-olympic-athletes/*

Note to parents and teachers:

Every effort has been made by the publisher to ensure that these websites contain no inappropriate or offensive material. However, because of the nature of the Internet, it is impossible to guarantee that the content of these sites will not be altered. We strongly advise that Internet access is supervised by a responsible adult.